A Child's History of Britain

Life in Roman Britain

Anita Ganeri

Raintree is an imprint of Capstone Global Library Limited, a company incorporated in England and Wales having its registered office at 7 Pilgrim Street, London, EC4V 6LB – Registered company number: 6695582

www.raintreepublishers.co.uk
myorders@raintreepublishers.co.uk

Edited by Nick Hunter and Penny West
Designed by Joanna Malivoire
Original illustration © Capstone Global Library Ltd 2014
Illustrated by: Laszlo Veres (pp.26-7), Beehive Illustration
Picture research by Mica Brancic
Originated by Capstone Global Library Ltd
Production by Helen McCreath
Printed and bound in China

ISBN 978 1 406 27048 8
18 17 16 15 14
10 9 8 7 6 5 4 3 2 1

British Library Cataloguing in Publication Data
A full catalogue record for this book is available from the British Library.

Acknowledgements
We would like to thank the following for permission to reproduce photographs: © The Trustees of British Museum p. 27 top; AKG-images pp. 24, 25; Alamy pp. 4 (© Robert Down), 9 (© The Art Archive/Gianni Dagli Orti), 10 (© Steve Vidler), 11 (© Linda Kennedy), 16 (© The Art Archive/Gianni Dagli Orti), 17 (© The Art Gallery Collection), 21 (© The Print Collector), 22 (© Ivy Close Images), 27 bottom (© Ancient Art & Architecture Collection Ltd/C M Dixon); Corbis p. 6 (© Heritage Images); Getty Images pp. 5 top (VisitBritain/Britain on View), 7 (Britain On View/Visit Britain/Rod Edwards), 12 (De Agostini//G. Dagli Orti), 13 (De Agostini/A Dagli Orti), 15 (De Agostini/A Dagli Orti), 18 (De Agostini/A Dagli Orti), 23 (Britain On View/Roger Coulam); Shutterstock pp. 5 bottom (© Shaun Jeffers), 19 (© tungtopgun), 20 (© My Good Images); The Picturedesk pp. 8 (Archaeological Museum Sofia/Dagli Orti), 14 (The Art Archive/Museum of London).

Cover photograph of a noblewoman playing a cithera reproduced with permission of The Bridgeman Art Library (Metropolitan Museum of Art, New York, USA).

We would like to thank Heather Montgomery for her invaluable help in the preparation of this book.

Every effort has been made to contact copyright holders of material reproduced in this book. Any omissions will be rectified in subsequent printings if notice is given to the publishers.

Disclaimer
All the Internet addresses (URLs) given in this book were valid at the time of going to press. However, due to the dynamic nature of the Internet, some addresses may have changed, or sites may have changed or ceased to exist since publication. While the author and Publishers regret any inconvenience this may cause readers, no responsibility for any such changes can be accepted by either the author or the Publishers.

Contents

Some words are shown in bold, **like this**. You can find out what they mean by looking in the glossary.

Who were the Romans?

More than 2,800 years ago, Rome was a group of small villages built on seven hills by the banks of the River Tiber in Italy. Over hundreds of years, it grew into a city at the centre of a mighty **empire**. The people of Rome conquered Italy and the lands around the Mediterranean Sea. These Romans also invaded France (Gaul) and Britain.

These are the ruins of the Roman amphitheatre at Caerleon (Isca) in South Wales.

ROMAN RULE

55 and 54 BC	Julius Caesar invades Britain
AD 43	Romans invade Britain
AD 61	Boudicca leads a revolt against the Romans
AD 84	The Romans have conquered almost all of Britain
AD 122	Romans build Hadrian's Wall to mark the edge of their empire
AD 410	End of Roman rule in Britain

Julius Caesar led two invasions of Britain, in 55 and 54 BC. Tribes of ancient Britons fought bravely against the Roman soldiers. Both times, the Romans went home. They returned in AD 43, and went on to rule Britain for almost 400 years.

This is a modern-day reenactment of a Roman army going into battle.

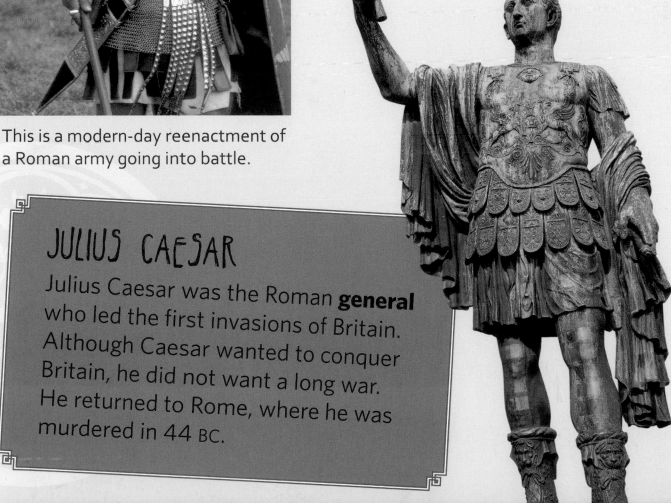

JULIUS CAESAR

Julius Caesar was the Roman **general** who led the first invasions of Britain. Although Caesar wanted to conquer Britain, he did not want a long war. He returned to Rome, where he was murdered in 44 BC.

Roman Britain

Before the Romans, the Celtic people of Britain lived in small villages and forts, built on hilltops. Their houses were made from wood and **thatch**.

The Romans built towns with houses, shops, markets, and workshops. They used stone and brick for their buildings. They also built paved roads between the towns. Some Roman towns had public baths and theatres.

By AD 100, London (Londinium) was the largest town in Britain. Chester (Castra Deva) was an important Roman fort. It had the biggest **amphitheatre** in Britain, which was used for training soldiers and for **gladiator** fights.

The palace of the Roman governor of London might have looked like this.

Here Is part of Hadrian's Wall near Housestead's Fort in Northumberland.

Hadrian's Wall

The Romans conquered the land that is now England and Wales by about AD 80. In AD 84, the Romans defeated an army in Scotland but then left Scotland again. In AD 122, **Emperor** Hadrian built a wall between England and Scotland to mark the edge of the Roman **Empire**.

ROMAN COINS

Roman coins had a picture of the emperor on one side. Some coins also had a picture of a woman wearing a long robe and holding a spear and shield. This was Britannia, the Roman name for Britain.

What would my family be like?

If you were a child in Roman Britain, your father would be the head of your family. He was expected to treat you fairly, but you had to obey him. For boys, childhood ended when you were 14 and were allowed to wear an adult **toga**. However, fathers were allowed to punish their children until they were 25 years old!

This scene is of a Roman family eating a banquet.

LIFE AND DEATH

A Roman father had great power in his family. When a baby was born, he decided whether to keep the baby or not. Sick babies, or those that the family could not afford to keep, were sometimes left outside to die, or to be picked up by someone else.

This slave is serving his owner a drink.

Slave labour

Your mother ran your home and looked after the children. If your family was wealthy, you had slaves to help. Slaves were often prisoners of war. They belonged to their owners and did not get paid for their work.

Getting married

Girls in Roman Britain were often married by the age of 14. Your parents arranged your marriage for you. Sons lived with their parents even after they got married.

Where would I live?

This is a beautiful mosaic from Fishbourne Palace in Sussex.

Life in Roman Britain was very different depending on whether you were rich or poor. If your family was wealthy, you lived in a grand house made of stone and tiles. In the countryside, these houses were called villas. Villas were usually built round a central courtyard, and had many different rooms. The walls were decorated with paintings, and there were tiles or **mosaics** on the floor.

In towns, poor people lived and worked in crowded houses. The room facing the street was a shop or workshop. The whole family lived, ate, and slept in a small back room. In the countryside, you probably lived in a small, round hut. The walls were made from woven pieces of wood, called wattle, covered with a sticky mixture of mud and straw, called daub. The huts had no windows, so they were dark and smoky from the cooking fire.

CENTRAL HEATING

Some wealthy Romans had central heating in their houses. Fires were lit under the ground-level floor, which was raised up on stacks of tiles. The heat spread under the floor and heated the rooms above.

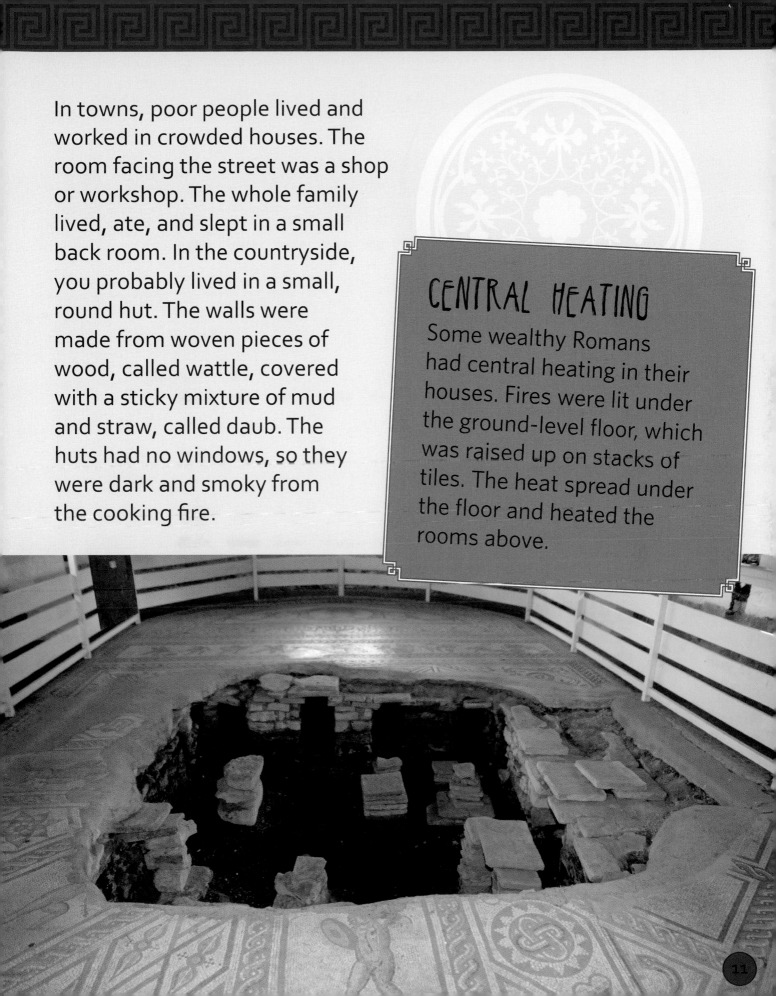

What clothes would I wear?

In Roman Britain, boys wore short knee-length tunics made from wool. The Romans thought only savages wore trousers! Girls wore longer tunics with woollen belts, tied around the waist.

To keep warm outdoors, girls and boys wore woollen cloaks that were fastened at the neck. Many people wore shoes made from leather.

This Roman girl is wearing a tunic with a belt around her waist.

If you came from a wealthy family, you could start wearing an adult **toga** when you were 14. A toga was a long piece of woollen cloth that you wore over your tunic. You kept it for special occasions. When girls got married, they were allowed to wear a stola. This was a long tunic fastened on the shoulders with clasps.

LUCKY CHARMS

A bulla was a lucky charm that Roman boys wore around their necks. A rich boy's bulla was made from gold. It was believed to protect him from evil spirits. When he became an adult, a boy gave up his bulla at a special ceremony.

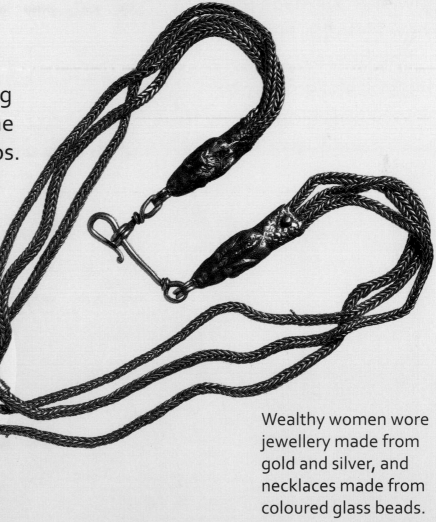

Wealthy women wore jewellery made from gold and silver, and necklaces made from coloured glass beads.

What would I eat and drink?

If your family was poor, you often only had just enough food to live. You ate bread, vegetables, and a tasteless porridge made from wheat. You sometimes had meat or fish if you went hunting or fishing. In towns, many poor people did not have anywhere to cook. They bought hot food from shops to eat at home.

Here is a model of a Roman kitchen, with utensils and pots for storing oil and wine.

FARMING

In the countryside, people grew crops, such as wheat, oats, barley, and vegetables. They kept cows, sheep, pigs, and goats for milk and meat. Children from poor families were expected to look after the animals from about the age of six.

People came from all over the Roman **Empire** to Britain. They brought many new foods with them, including carrots, cucumbers, olives, and figs. Rich Romans ate plenty of meat, especially "sucking pig" or piglets. They also loved seafood, such as mussels and oysters.

In this carving, a wealthy Roman woman is enjoying a banquet. Her slave is nearby.

Roman feasts

Wealthy Romans held banquets where people lay on couches to eat. They propped themselves up on one elbow and ate with the other hand. Slaves served the food and wine. The food enjoyed by wealthy Romans included peacocks, ostriches, thrushes, and roasted dormice, dipped in honey.

Would I go to school?

Poor Roman children did not go to school. Their parents could not afford to send them. Instead, they were expected to help their parents with their work. Some boys learnt a craft, such as woodworking or making **mosaics**. Girls learnt how to run a household.

This is a stone carving of Roman boys and their teacher.

Children in Roman Britain did not have books to write in. A pupil used a metal pointer, called a stylus, to write on a small wax tablet.

Most schools were in towns. If your family were wealthy and you were a boy, you might go to a *ludus*, or primary school, from the age of six. You learnt reading, writing, and arithmetic (maths). At 11 or 12, some boys went on to a *grammaticus*, or grammar school. There, you learnt history and public speaking so that you could work in law or in government. Many children from wealthy families had home tutors. These teachers were often educated slaves.

LEARNING LATIN

The Romans' language was called Latin. In Roman Britain, children learnt Latin at school. But in everyday life, most people still spoke their own language, such as one of the Celtic languages.

How would I have fun?

In Roman Britain, rich children played with rag dolls, wooden soldiers, and animals made from wood or clay. You also had marbles, yo-yos, and skipping ropes. Some wealthy children had wooden dolls with movable arms and legs. If you were poor, you probably did not have much time to play!

The Romans loved to play dice and knucklebones. Knucklebones was played with the small bones from a sheep or goat. The player threw the bones up, then scored points depending on which way they landed.

These Roman toys are carved in the shape of animals.

Bloody sports

Chariot racing and **gladiator** fights were very popular in Roman times. Chariot races were held on tracks called circuses. People went to **amphitheatres** to watch gladiator fights. The gladiators were often criminals or slaves. At the end of a fight, the defeated gladiator might be killed. Sometimes, gladiators had to fight wild animals.

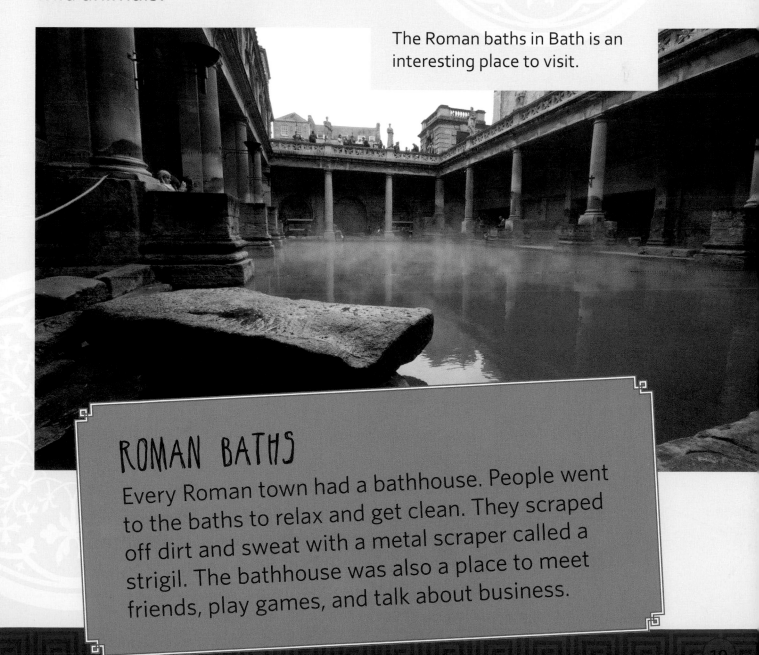

The Roman baths in Bath is an interesting place to visit.

ROMAN BATHS

Every Roman town had a bathhouse. People went to the baths to relax and get clean. They scraped off dirt and sweat with a metal scraper called a strigil. The bathhouse was also a place to meet friends, play games, and talk about business.

What would I believe?

Before the Romans arrived, the ancient Britons worshipped their own gods and goddesses. They believed that many of these spirits lived in places such as springs, rivers, and forests.

The Romans brought their own religion to Britain. They also worshipped many gods and goddesses. Each god or goddess looked after different people or events. The Romans built temples and **sacrificed** animals as offerings to the gods.

Neptune was god of the sea.

Mixing it up

Over time, these two religions were mixed together in Britain. In Bath, for example, a hot spring was home to the ancient goddess Sulis. The Romans linked Sulis to their own goddess Minerva. They encouraged people to worship at the spring, and they built a temple and baths there.

This is a Roman mosaic of Jesus Christ, from a villa in Dorset.

In the 1st century AD, many Romans began to **convert** to the new religion of Christianity. This religion spread across the Roman **Empire** and arrived in Britain by the AD 200s.

SOME ROMAN GODS AND GODDESSES

Jupiter – king of the gods; god of thunder and lightning

Mars – god of war

Apollo – god of the sun

Mercury – messenger of the gods

Minerva – goddess of wisdom and learning

Venus – goddess of love and beauty

Who joined the army?

The Roman army was extremely well organized. They fought wars against Rome's enemies, and conquered foreign lands. They also kept strict control over Roman territories, such as Britain.

This is a Roman legionary.

Life in the legions

You could join the Roman army from the age of 17, although many boys were younger than that. If you joined the army, your life was very tough. You were expected to march over 30 kilometres (19 miles) a day. You had to carry all your equipment and weapons, as well as wear heavy armour.

There were the two kinds of soldier in the Roman army. You could be a legionary or an auxiliary. A legionary was a Roman **citizen**. Highly trained legionaries were usually in the army for 20 to 25 years.

Auxiliary army

Auxiliaries came from places that had been conquered by the Romans. Auxiliaries earned less money than legionaries did. One of their main jobs was to defend the **frontiers** of the Roman **Empire,** such as the forts along Hadrian's Wall.

ENGINEERS AND BUILDERS

Roman legionaries were trained for fighting. But they were also engineers and builders. They built roads and forts, as well as structures such as Hadrian's Wall.

Here is a model of the gatehouse to a fort on Hadrian's Wall.

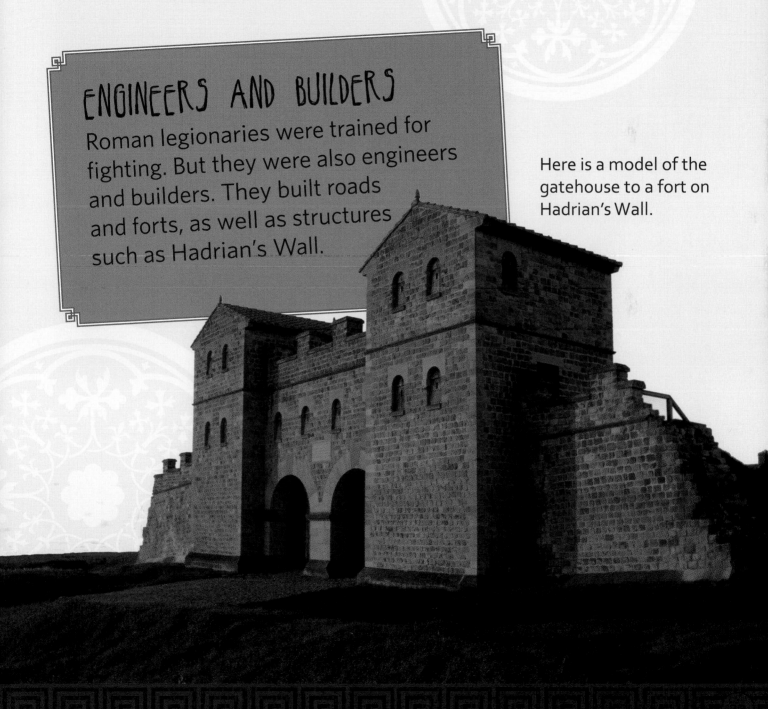

After the Romans

This picture shows the last Roman emperor handing over power in 476.

By the year **AD** 400, the Romans had ruled Britain for more than 350 years. Many people in Britain lived a Roman lifestyle and thought of themselves as Roman. However, the Roman **Empire** was becoming weak and there were arguments about who should be **emperor**. Enemies from outside the empire began to attack and threaten Roman lands.

Britain came under threat from people called the Anglo-Saxons. They came from Germany, Denmark, and Holland. They sailed across the North Sea, looking for new lands to settle in. The Romans built forts along the south coast of England to defend themselves from the Anglo-Saxons. But in 410, the Roman legionaries left Britain and went back to defend Rome. This marked the end of Roman rule in Britain.

People could no longer make a living in the Roman towns. They went back to the countryside and gave up their Roman way of life. Gradually, the Anglo-Saxons took over large parts of Britain.

This painting shows Anglo-Saxon ships landing in England.

BURIED TREASURE

When the Romans left, many wealthy people buried their jewellery and money in the ground to keep it safe from the Anglo-Saxons. They hoped to dig it up again when things were safer.

How do we know?

The ruined fort of Vindolanda lies close to Hadrian's Wall in Northumberland. For hundreds of years, it was home to the Roman soldiers, and their families, who guarded the border of northern England. **Archaeologists** began to investigate the fort in the 1930s. They have found the remains of a bathhouse, houses, workshops, and bathrooms, along with thousands of everyday objects, such as coins, combs, bowls, shoes, and letters.

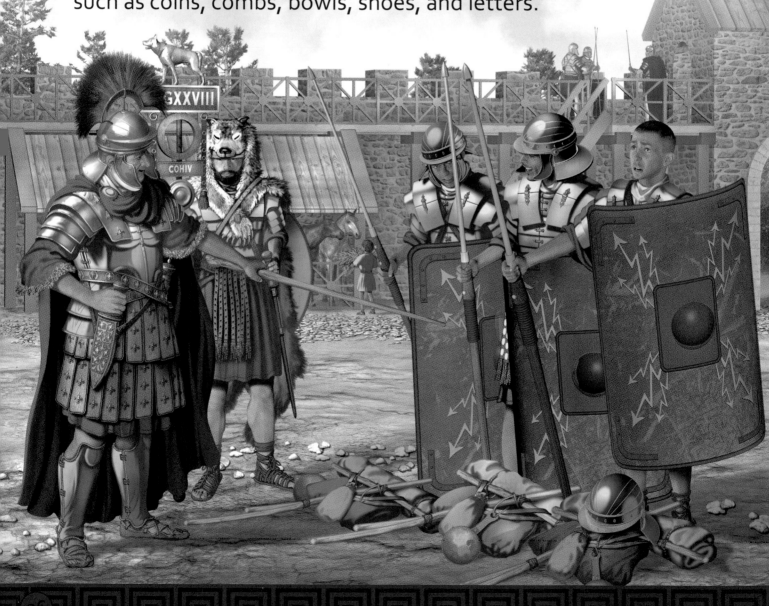

This is a letter from one Roman woman to another, inviting her to a birthday party. It was written in ink on a wooden tablet and is in Latin. It was found at the Vindolanda fort, south of Hadrian's Wall.

This is a leather sandal worn by a legionary. It was found in York.

Map

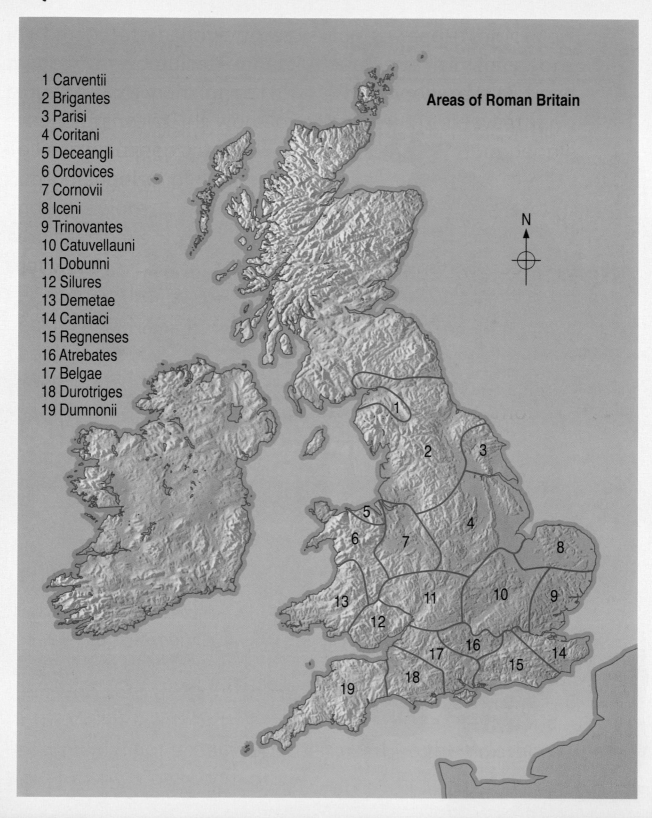

1 Carventii
2 Brigantes
3 Parisi
4 Coritani
5 Deceangli
6 Ordovices
7 Cornovii
8 Iceni
9 Trinovantes
10 Catuvellauni
11 Dobunni
12 Silures
13 Demetae
14 Cantiaci
15 Regnenses
16 Atrebates
17 Belgae
18 Durotriges
19 Dumnonii

Areas of Roman Britain

Quiz

What do you know about life in Roman Britain? Try this quiz to find out!

1. Who wore trousers in the Roman Empire?
   a wealthy men
   b no one – the Romans thought they were for savages
   c poor men

2. How did wealthy Romans eat their dinner?
   a lying on couches
   b sitting around a long table
   c standing up

3. How did Roman children practise their writing?
   a copying words into a book
   b writing on a slate
   c writing with a stylus on wax

4. What was a strigil?
   a something used for picking out ear wax
   b something used for eating food
   c something used for scraping off dirt and sweat

5. What did gladiators do?
   a build Roman central heating systems
   b fight in amphitheatres
   c teach in Roman schools

Answers
1. b
2. a
3. c
4. c
5. b

29

Glossary

AD dates after the birth of Christ; these count upwards, so AD 20 is earlier than AD 25

amphitheatre open-air theatre with seats on rising steps surrounding a stage

archaeologist person who finds and studies places and objects from the past

BC dates before the birth of Christ; these count downwards, so 25 BC is earlier than 20 BC

citizen in Roman times, a Roman citizen had special rights and privileges in the empire

convert change belief or religious faith

emperor person that rules an empire

empire group of states and territories under the rule of one country

frontier border between one country and another

general person in charge of an army

gladiator man trained to fight with weapons against other men or wild animals in an amphitheatre

mosaic picture made up from lots of small pieces of coloured tile, stone, or glass

sacrifice give something to please a god or goddess

toga piece of cloth wrapped loosely around the body

thatch roof made from straw

Find out more

Books

100 Facts Roman Britain, Philip Steele (Miles Kelly, 2008)

Men, Women and Children in Roman Britain, Jane Bingham (Wayland, 2011)

Roman Britain (History on Your Doorstep), Alex Woolf (Franklin Watts, 2012)

The Romans in Britain, Brian Knapp (Atlantic Europe Publishing, 2010)

The Usborne Official Roman Soldier's Handbook, Lesley Sims (Usborne, 2009)

What the Romans Did for Us, Alison Hawes (A&C Black, 2009)

Websites

www.bbc.co.uk/schools/primaryhistory/romans
This BBC history website has facts, activities, and lots more about Roman Britain.

www.britishmuseum.org/explore/cultures/europe/roman_britain.aspx
There are many Roman artefacts to discover on the British Museum website.

www.museumoflondon.org.uk/learning/features_facts/digging
Visit the Museum of London's website to find out more about life in Roman times, particularly in London (Londinium).

www.vindolanda.com
Discover the Roman fort of Vindolanda and find out about the people who lived there.

Places to visit

There are many Roman sites to visit all over Britain. You can find out about them through the following organizations:

English Heritage
www.english-heritage.org.uk

The National Trust in England, Wales, and Northern Ireland
www.nationaltrust.org.uk

Index